# The PARENT TRAP



CRYSTAL WRIGHT ADAMS

ISBN 979-8-88832-744-9 (paperback)
ISBN 979-8-88832-745-6 (digital)



Christian Faith Publishing
832 Park Avenue
Meadville, PA 16335
www.christianfaithpublishing.com

All Scripture references are taken from *The Holy Bible: New International Version* unless otherwise noted. Biblica, Inc., 2011.

Printed in the United States of America

# ACKNOWLEDGMENTS

To my amigos,

The two of you are the most important people in my life. You are my gift. You are my reward. You are my heritage. Everything I do in this life is to make your lives better. Everything I do in this world is to make it worthy of containing the two of you. You are my inspiration and my motivation. You make me a better mother, a better sister, a better daughter, a better leader, a better woman and a better human being. You are the reasons for this book. I thank God for using you both to show me a better way for us, the three amigos! I pray that this journey we've taken together will blaze the trail for the generations that follow after.

Love you more,
Mom

# CONTENTS

# The Trap Is Set

I have not come across a single parent who, at one time or another, didn't feel completely ill-equipped for the vocation of parenthood. Raising tiny humans to be larger humans who are kind, selfless, and possess a sense of duty to make the world they inherited from us better is a lot of responsibility! I mean, there have been some days during this COVID-19 quarantine that I may have neglected to brush *my own* teeth, yet I'm expected, entrusted even, to raise a world changer? Make it make sense, Jesus! Can I get an *amen*? What makes this task even harder is the lack of specific instruction and the vast amount of professional and pseudoprofessional opinions on the topic of parenting—"Don't coddle your child when they cry, or you'll make them codependent!" "Be sure to nurture your child when they cry, or they'll turn into sociopaths." Being a parent today often means that everything you do *right* is also completely *wrong*. Some days it feels like a complete and total trap, but what I've learned in the trenches of parenthood (because this is a battlefield and we're at war, whether in the natural or spiritual) is what has worked for another parent, even my own parents, does not necessarily work for me.

If you've been a parent for more than five minutes, you know as well as I do that there's no manual for this. Wouldn't that be nice? Alas, there's no book of instruction on how to perfectly raise children, and this one is most certainly *not* it. What I want to explore in this book is some of the parenting philosophies I was raised by and how, for me, they weren't the *right* way to parent my own kids.

I'm guessing that if you're reading this book, you've had your own experiences with some of these philosophies. I'm also hoping that sharing some of my personal experiences will allow you to rest in the truth that when it comes to parenting, there is no one-size-fits-all approach. There's also no such thing as perfect, so let's just throw that one out with the bathwater too (but save the baby)! If you're a parent, you're going to mess up; you're going to make mistakes. Like Thanos, it is inevitable. So instead of trying to uphold the illusion that you have it all together and/or being peer-pressured into parenting in a way that doesn't work for your children, just lean into the imperfection and commit to finding the way that best works for you and your kiddos. God is not looking for perfection. He doesn't have to because He is perfect. He's looking for willing hearts and He would not have trusted us with the specific children He gave us if He hadn't already equipped us to steward them well.

The Bible says that there is a way that seems right to a man, but its end is the way to death (Proverbs 14:12). Now don't be alarmed! I'm not saying parenting the *wrong* way will cause your child to die. What I am saying is parenting your child in a way that's wrong for them can lead to the death of their peace, strength, and confidence— and sometimes yours. It's true there is no manual on parenting, but we do have another book of instruction we can consult: the Bible. I'm sure all my fellow Sunday School and Vacation Bible School alums learned this acrostic for the Bible when we were our kids' ages: Basic Instructions Before Leaving Earth. As Christians, the Bible is our manual. As parents, the Bible is a powerful guide to help us navigate parenthood by ensuring the parenting philosophies we utilize with our children are aligned with the principles of our heavenly Father (Proverbs 16:9). What would Jesus do? That should be the forethought in our minds as we rear our children. That's not to say that you can't learn from other parents in your life or gain wisdom through their experiences. If that weren't true, there would be no reason for me to write this book. I'm simply saying that just because your momma, daddy, granny, and big momma did it that way doesn't mean it's the right and only way for you. Remember, no parent is perfect, and our parents are no exception.

There were certain parenting philosophies I grew up under and tried to apply with my kids that threatened to kill my patience and peace and theirs too. I had to make the decision to either do what had always been done or try something different. Trying something different hasn't always been easy and has been far from perfect. Trying something different also invites the potential judgment and disapproval of others, especially those who believe what has always been done is *right*. However, trying something different has worked better for me and my kids than anything I've tried before. Remember, this is a battlefield, and the enemy is coming for our kids just like he comes for us. Don't let him use you as a weapon in his arsenal. When you have the choice to pick your battles in this war, pick what works best for you and your child. If that choice is grounded in the Word, God will honor that, and you will see victory in one way or another. So in the words of the great philosopher Captain Steve Rogers, "Parents, assemble!"

# CHAPTER 1

# Because I Said So!

Okay… I know I've probably already triggered some of you. Trust me, I get it. It's the parental retort that haunts more than a few of our childhood memories. What was most impressive about my mom's wielding of this phrase was the versatility with which she used it. As a child, *because I said so* was often the explanation given to me when I questioned my parents' response or decision to my question or request; usually this response or decision was, "No." Though it typically followed a no, this phrase had unlimited applications. Why can't I have dessert? *Because I said so!* Why can't I stay up late? *Because I said so!* Why can't I go to my friend's house? *Because I said so!* Why can't I do my homework later? *Because I said so!* Why do I have to do this chore? *Because I said so!* Why should I buy another copy of this book to gift to a friend? *Because I said so*! Okay, maybe not that last one. I was just checking to make sure you were paying attention. *Because I said so* wasn't just a reply, it was often the end of the conversation. The problem with that is when we don't give our children a chance to question things or we don't adequately explain our reasons, we rob them of prime opportunities to develop critical thinking skills and understand the consequences for their actions.

Too little explanation or giving unclear or ambiguous answers to even the simplest questions can leave our children feeling uncertain and confused. For some children, that lack of clarity brings automatic resistance. It's not that they desire to be openly defiant or rebellious, but they do desire to have a sense of understanding and consequently a sense of control in their world. Why is this boundary important? For other children, this phrase hinders their ability to think for themselves. Stopping the conversation with *because I said so* prevents the cognitive process of analyzing a situation and understanding its best course of action from taking place. It can also prevent them from learning how to set and maintain healthy boundaries for themselves. Don't just take my word for it. Let's see what our manual (*the* Word) says.

The Bible is filled with stories and instructions that detail and lay out certain boundaries God has given us and why they're important or good for us. Every boundary, command, or directive God gives us in His Word is designed to keep us from spiritual, emotional, mental, physical, financial, or relational harm—to lead us to His best for us. This is the same thing we endeavor to do for our children. In Genesis chapter 2, God gave His first child here on earth one of the most consequential boundaries any child has ever been given: "But you must not eat from the tree of the knowledge of good and evil" (Genesis 2:17). He didn't stop there. God didn't say not to eat from the tree *because He said so!* He explained to Adam that eating from that tree would lead to his death, and it did. Cut to Genesis chapter 3 and we very quickly see the consequences of Adam and Eve violating God's only boundary for them: banishment from paradise and forfeiting eternal life a.k.a. death (Genesis 3:23). Now I know what you're thinking, "Crystal, this example proves that even when the parent gave a full explanation of the boundary He set and clearly articulated the consequences, the children still violated it." You're right. The outcomes of these situations are rarely dependent on one factor. It is very possible that if God's directive had ended with *because I said so,* Adam and Eve would never have violated that boundary. Anything is possible. However, not everything is probable. When you are setting boundaries for your children, such as bedtimes, no more sweets, chores, and what they aren't permitted to do, explaining why the boundary is important for them—and sometimes even you—leads to a higher probability that it will be understood and honored…and then there's free will. God gave Adam and Eve the power to choose if they would obey or not. We have been given that same power, and so have our children. Free will is a gift, but it comes with consequences whether good or bad. Even the most heartfelt explanation of why a boundary has been set does not mean it won't be violated. As parents, when our explanation does not produce the expected outcome, we are presented with another choice: How will we respond? Do we go back to what we've always known? How our parents responded? When our kids don't meet our expectations, we tend to think it's a "them" problem, but that perception is rooted in the expectations that were placed on us as children.

I heard *because I said so* more times than I can remember as a child. Though I was very compliant, I have always possessed a need to understand the *why*. This included the why behind the rules, regulations, and boundaries my parents set for me and my siblings. My mom used *because I said so* early and so often that I got to the point of no longer asking why. I knew no real explanation would be given anyway, so it was easier to just accept this response. Questioning my parents could also be viewed as disrespect in my household, and I knew the consequences of that action all too well. Not being able to ask and understand why, as a child, had some detrimental effects on me as young adult. I had been conditioned to accept a lack of explanation even if I didn't like it or it didn't make sense to me. That learned behavior led me down a long and often heartbreaking road of accepting things at face value even when my intuition was telling me to dig deeper or gain more understanding. That same road eventually brought me to parenthood. Save for the lack of sleep (can we talk about how no one warns you about that? Maybe in the next book...stay focused), parenting my first child was pretty easy. He is sweet, uber intelligent, kind-hearted, sharp as a whip, a master builder, and a very compliant child. When you set a boundary for him, he will adhere to it often with no complaints or questions. "Yes, ma'am," is typically his only response. He's also the kind of child that self-governs and will adhere to the boundary even when there is no one around to police him. My second child? He is the inspiration for my coining of the phrase "second child syndrome." I know you may think you came up with that one, but trust me, my second-born son is its origin. There's something about that second child that God sees as a perfect opportunity to prune you and make you more like Him. Can any of you relate? Becoming pregnant while I was on birth control should have been enough of a warning for me. My second child came out of the womb bucking the status quo. He is fierce, a protector, a creative, extremely caring, a math wizard, and endlessly inquisitive. It was when he was only three years old that he started to find his voice and started questioning mine…and everything else.

Any boundary I set seemed like a personal challenge to him. In the frustration of dealing with these challenges, I started to revert to what I had learned growing up. "Why can't I stay up and watch TV until 11 pm at night?" *Because I said so, little three-year-old boy!* (I jazzed mine up a bit, but you know you're done when you start adding *little* and your kid's age into your replies.) Want to guess how that went over? See, I was initially just as inquisitive as he was when I was little. I asked a lot of questions, but I was made to believe questioning a boundary my parents set was disrespectful. I applied that same perspective to my son questioning mine. The difference was that he didn't relent. No matter how many times I said *because I said so*, or even when the consequences became more serious for his continued questioning of me, he never stopped asking. The outcome here was that *I* was the one who started to feel like I had no control over my world. I couldn't even get my three-year-old to comply with a simple boundary. I felt judged by other parents, including my own, and, very transparently, I started to resent my son because his older brother never gave me those problems. Obviously, the issue was with him, right? I was at my wit's end and feeling helpless when the Holy Spirit nudged me and said, "Give him to Me." That night, instead of praying that God change this child He gave me, I prayed that He would help me become the parent my child needed me to be for him. Part of this transformational process meant acknowledging that parenting philosophies like *because I said so* did not work for me or my kids, at least not for my youngest son. I would have to give my kids the respect of explaining why, and often more than once, if I wanted them to truly understand and respect the boundary. Dr. Emerson Eggerichs says that when we instruct our kids on various topics, we must get at the why and explain the reasons behind the teaching.[1] I had to shift my perspective from one of exerting authority over my kids and/or registering them asking questions of me as disrespect, to that of realizing my job as their parent was to explain and help them learn, understand, and grow—to give them the tools to better engage with the world around them, raise them up in the way they should go (Proverbs 22:6). If they couldn't gain that understanding in the safety of their own home with their loving parent, how would they ever?

I also had to learn that a violation of my boundary was not a personal affront to me. It was just an opportunity for further explanation, reinforcement, and allowing my kids to learn that their actions had consequences. Sticking to appropriate consequences for the violation was crucial here. When my son would beg me not to enforce the consequences he earned after repeated explanations and violations of a boundary, I would say something like, "Mommy loves you very much. Your behavior today has shown me that you are not able to handle [insert privilege here], but Mommy has full faith in you that tomorrow you'll have the behavior necessary to keep your [privilege]." I can't remember what book I learned this from, and it seems like a mouthful, but it was highly effective for me and my youngest son. Fully explaining the *why* and sticking to the appropriate consequences (I can't stress this part enough) when necessary, created a whole new channel of dialogue for not only me and him but also for me and my oldest son. Seeing the change in my response empowered my first son to ask why and question things that didn't make sense to him. This gave me the opportunity to help him gain understanding too. Now I would be lying if I said there wasn't still the occasional time where my response to my children is, "Sometimes the answer is just because Mommy said so." However, this is always a last resort and never a first response. The foundation of trust and communication that has been built between us has allowed them to ultimately accept that application of *because I said so.*

---

[1]   See Dr. Emerson Eggerichs, *Love & Respect in the Family* (Nashville: W Publishing Group, 2013) 80.

So if you're like me and were raised by the *because I said so* philosophy, I challenge you to really evaluate the effects it had on you and how successful you have been with continuing this philosophy with your own children. If it's not working for you like it didn't work for me, I encourage you to find a different way that works better for you and your kids. I promise it will bring you much more peace and a more open line of communication with your children, and that's not just because I said so!

# CHAPTER 2

# Do as I Say, Not as I Do

As you can see, we're continuing with the A-side hits. *Do as I say not as I do* was an instant classic in many of our childhoods. The unique thing about this particular parenting philosophy is that it wasn't always verbalized. As the saying would suggest, this philosophy was often modeled by our parents. For example, some of us may have witnessed our parents using foul language toward others or even experienced them using it toward us when they were upset or angry. However, if we were found using that same language, we were punished. If we dared to try and point out the hypocrisy, it would garner another *do as I say not as I do* response, if not graver consequences. Like *because I said so*, *do as I say not as I do* was highly versatile. Did you ever wonder why it was okay for Dad to devour a whole bag of chips before dinner but a snack would ruin your appetite? Did you ever ponder on why it was okay for Mom to gossip about someone on the phone but you calling someone a "bad name" was unbecoming? Did you ever think about why it was okay for your parents to throw verbal punches at each other in front of you but fighting with your sibling would earn you a lecture, grounding, or even a spanking? These and other questions from our childhoods were very succinctly addressed by *do as I say not as I do*. The problem with the dichotomy of this philosophy is that when it comes to children, more is caught than taught. This is to say that the actions you model far outweigh the instructions you give or expectations you set verbally. Dr.

Emerson Eggerichs says that "the power of example is incalculable."[2] Instructing your kids is of little effect unless you model what you tell them. Regardless of what you say, it's your actions that have the most impact. Our manual, the Bible, offers many great examples of this.

The book of Titus is a letter to a mentee named Titus from his mentor, the apostle Paul. We can apply the dynamics of this mentor-mentee relationship to our parent-child relationships. Paul served as someone entrusted to provide guidance, instruction, encouragement, and support (covering) to Titus as he worked to spread the gospel and establish the church in Crete. In his letter, Paul gives detailed instructions to Titus on how to identify perspective leaders for the new church. Titus was warned not to just listen to their words but to vet their actions: "They claim to know God, but by their actions they deny Him. They are detestable, disobedient and unfit for doing any good." (Titus 1:16) As a parent, two things jump out at me from this scripture. First is that Paul himself would have had to model this leadership in Titus's life for Titus to both understand the instruction and to apply it during the vetting process. Second is how crucial (or incalculable) their leaders' righteous actions and behaviors were in establishing the church. In the body of Christ, the church is not a building you meet at once a week. It is a group of believers coming together to fulfill a common purpose. The church is like a family. Paul's instruction to Titus highlights that the leaders of the family must set the right example through their actions.

Paul goes on to say that the leaders who don't set the right example are detestable, disobedient, and unfit for doing any good. Now let me pause here and clarify something. I am not calling any person that has used the *do as I say not as I do* philosophy those things. Whether it was our parents using it on us or us using it on our own children, I don't believe that makes anyone a bad person. Where I will draw the connection is when we, as parents, fail to have our actions match our words, or worse, place expectations on our children that we ourselves are not accountable to; we are teaching them that as long as they say

---

[2]   See Dr. Emerson Eggerichs, *Love & Respect in the Family* (Nashville: W Publishing Group, 2013) 82.

the right things, they don't have to live them. People governed by this type of philosophy may follow the "wrong" example being modeled, which could lead to failure in accomplishing the purpose of the body. After all, purpose requires action.

To be very transparent, *do as I say not as I do* is one of the parenting philosophies caught in my childhood that I struggle the most with as a parent. It's so easy to fall into because it's often nonverbally executed. I don't think I've ever actually told my sons to *do as I say not as I do*, but I know without a shadow of a doubt that I've employed this philosophy on several occasions. You know, like telling them they can't have any more sweets for the day as I'm stuffing a handful of M&Ms into my mouth. Sound familiar? No judgment from me! I asked my eight-and-a-half-year-old and almost ten-year-old sons if they could recall a time when I told them to do something but my actions were opposite. I was sure they would bring up the M&Ms or maybe my festive choice of words while encouraging my fellow drivers on the road. Their responses surprised me a bit (side note: It's amazing what our kids will share with us if we just ask and give them a safe space to answer honestly. Okay, back to the regularly scheduled program). My oldest son revealed that it annoys him when I'm constantly rushing him to hurry up and get ready to leave the house, but then I keep them waiting at the door while I'm texting on my phone. Well…he's not wrong, and while this particular example may seem inconsequential compared to bad words, poor diet habits, and gossiping, I would disagree.

The fact of the matter is that my son has heard me express an expectation of him, often vocalized in frustration, and then seen me act completely opposite. The more I think about that, it's no coincidence that I have had an increasingly hard time getting him out the door in the morning. Remember, my oldest son is my compliant child. He's also very much a morning person. So when I ask him if his hair and teeth are brushed, shoes are on, and he's ready to go, and he responds yes not having done any of those things, he's not lying—he's following my example. I think this is the first time I've ever had an epiphany about my own behavior *while* writing about it. Thank you for attending my TED Talk! Seriously though, while my words are saying, "You need to get ready and let's go!" my actions are saying that we obviously have time to do what *I* want to do. My son says it annoys him, but I suspect it also makes him feel devalued and like his wants are not as important. If they were, I would hold myself accountable to the same expectations I have of him. His behavioral response is the result of those feelings. This affects my younger son, too. Though I typically no longer have issues with him getting ready in the morning, my nagging of his brother tends to cause him frustration. He seems to vacillate between being upset with the tone I'm using with his brother and his brother's lack of compliance. My application of *do as I say not as I do* can disrupt our whole morning vibe and leave all three of us feeling a way.

If you're like me and have either consciously or subconsciously implemented the *do as I say not as I do* philosophy from your childhood into your parenting style, I encourage you to really evaluate the actions you display toward your children. Are you asking them to uphold a standard that you aren't? If you don't know, just ask! They will tell you if you give them the opportunity to do so without reacting negatively. Remember, as their parents, we set the example by our actions and reactions. You can be a thermometer or a thermostat. A thermometer simply responds to the conditions of its environment. Applying a parenting philosophy to your kids just because it's what you learned in your childhood environment is thermometer behavior. By contrast, a thermostat controls the atmosphere of its environment. Choosing to set an example for your kids that matches your verbalized expectations of *them* is big thermostat energy. If you choose the latter, they will be doing as you do, and there's a lot of good to be said of that!

# CHAPTER 3

# Children Should Be Seen and Not Heard

So this particular philosophy is one of the more antiquated ones; by today's standards it's a B-side classic. I can't say that I have ever heard my parents articulate this belief, but I do believe it's the foundation of one that I did hear from time to time growing up: "Don't speak unless you've been spoken to." This wasn't a phrase that was uttered solely by my parents. When I was growing up, *any* adult was empowered to exercise this philosophy (and many others) with the children in their care, custody, or control. As a child, and truthfully as an adult now, I could be described as a "talker." Don't let the length of my literary works fool you, ya' girl could and still can talk most people under the table. Whether it was asking questions, telling a story, talking to the TV, or even just talking aloud to myself, I could often be found keeping the conversation going. From a very young age, I was comfortable with and practiced in using my voice. My parents, however, were less comfortable with it. Don't get me wrong! Now that I'm a parent myself, I completely get it. My sons are their mothers' children. My oldest can talk me down even on my best day. He has my innate ability for storytelling, and like his mother, he leaves no detail out. His stories include a lot of explanation and very little room to respond. My youngest son? Well, I've heard it said that asking questions is a sign of genius. If that's true, my son would most certainly qualify for Mensa. There is no shortage of inquiries just waiting to fire in rapid succession from this kid's mind and mouth. Lately, he also has this really fun habit of asking a question and then interrupting you as you're replying so that he can answer the question first. Between the two of them, there are days that I just want to yell, "Shut up!" Quite honestly, there have been a few days when I have. In our household, it's two-on-one, and those odds can leave Mommy feeling exhausted and in need of some peace and quiet. So trust me, I understand. I'm also in agreement that our children need to learn how to find balance when it comes to their noise production. That, however, requires us as their parents not to classify their every audible emission as *noise*.

When I was a young girl and my parents were exhausted and in need of some peace and quiet, their response to my stories, questions, and general talking were things like this: "Would you wrap it up?" "Does this story have a point?" "Crys, I just got in the door. Can you give me a break? Be quiet!" and sometimes, "Would you just shut up!" I don't blame them. They just wanted a little quiet, and that's perfectly reasonable. Yet the message I was receiving was that *children should be seen and not heard.* Over time, that message became louder and clearer, especially when it came to my communication with my dad. Using my voice was at best annoying and at worst unimportant to him, so I didn't. This was never more evident than when attempting to defend myself during a lecture. Not only was I not permitted to speak, but the words I did get out were discredited. I had lost the power to use my voice. I went from being a young girl who would speak up in any situation to a young lady who felt compelled to keep everything bottled up inside. The problem with bottling things up is that they could eventually explode. Therein lies the danger of this particular parenting philosophy. It can condition your kids to shut down or blow up! As I recount my story, I can't help but think about another young lady's story from the Bible. Hers was a story about the power of using your voice.

The book of Esther introduces us to a beautiful young woman whose beauty and grace was so favored by the ruling king that she ultimately became queen, but Esther was keeping a secret. Before she left to go to the king's palace, her older cousin and guardian, Mordecai, instructed her not to reveal her Jewish heritage or family background to anyone. Before being made queen, Esther was put in the care of the king's eunuch, Hegai, who instructed her on what to ask of the king to win his favor, and she did. It wasn't long after Esther became queen that her cousin Mordecai overheard an assassination plot to kill the king. He alerted Esther who told the king, and the plot was foiled. Despite Mordecai's role in stopping the assassination, he later found himself at the center of another plot—to destroy all the Jews in the kingdom. Mordecai was distraught, and when Esther heard of this, she sent her eunuchs to find out why. Mordecai informed her of the plot to kill the Jews and sent instructions back to Esther to go before the king and beg for mercy for her people. Esther initially made excuses for why she couldn't do what Mordecai asked. She was afraid to go before the king without him sending for her because doing so could mean a death sentence for her. Mordecai replied to her, saying, "For if you remain silent at this time, relief and deliverance for the Jews will arise from another place, but you and your father's family will perish. And who knows but that you have come to your royal position for such a time as this?" (Esther 4:14). Hearing this, Esther wisely, strategically, and with much prayer and fasting, presented herself to the king. He called her into his presence and was so pleased with her that he said he would grant any request she asked of him, even up to half the kingdom. Empowered to use her voice, Esther asked for the lives of her and her people to be spared. The king not only granted her request, but the person who conspired to destroy the Jews was killed himself. A few things stand out to me in Esther's story.

First, Esther didn't exercise free rein in using her voice. Various times throughout her story, she was given advice or instructions (parameters) from other people she trusted on how to use her voice. In his book on relational intelligence, Dr. Dharius Daniels talks about the importance of advisors. An advisor is someone who provides covering to their advisee. They must be like an umbrella which prevents unnecessary exposure and not a lid which limits and contains.[3] The practice of using her voice strategically is what prepared her for the second thing that stood out to me. Esther being empowered to use her voice was the difference between life and death for both her and many others. The same is true metaphorically for our children.

When we limit, control, or outright silence our children's voices by operating under the *children should be seen and not heard* philosophy, we are potentially robbing them of fulfilling the purpose for which they were created—for such a time as this. I once heard T. D. Jakes say that the reason he became a preacher or speaker was because his mother let him talk. When she was in the kitchen making dinner or doing some other tasks, she would listen as he told his stories and asked his questions. That really struck me. It was the first time I was truly confronted with how I was responding to my sons when they did the same. I know without a shadow of a doubt that my sons were created to be leaders and affect positive change on this earth, but was it possible that I was unknowingly containing what God purposed them for because I wanted a little peace and quiet? I really had to examine myself.

If you've ever found yourself asking the same questions as me, it should be clear to you by now that you're not alone. Children can be loud and highly inquisitive—at least that runs in my family. I don't ever want to limit my children in a way that causes them to lose their voice. I do, however, think creating parameters for your child and communicating those parameters clearly and positively is not only necessary but also brings a balance for both them and you. Instead of just shutting them down, try giving them a set amount of time to tell their story. That way, you won't feel bombarded coming through the door. You're mentally prepared and teaching them how to be more concise. Another idea is having a designated time for stories. Maybe turning the TV off during dinner and giving your children the time and freedom to express themselves can help to create that balance. I think it's also helpful to really think about what *you* might

---

[3] See Dr. Dharius Daniels, *Relational Intelligence* (Grand Rapids: Zondervan, 2020) 78.

be doing while your kids are talking that's adding to the frustration. Are you doing taxes or scrolling through social media? Either way, you have the choice to pause and give your kids your attention or clearly communicate that you need a set amount of time to finish your task and then listen to what they have to say or answer their question. The key here is being accountable to the time frame you gave them. These are just a few techniques I've implemented with my sons that have worked for us. Whatever techniques you choose, keep them clear, positive, and always allowing for your child to use their voice. If you do, you may see less blowups or shutdowns from them and experience more peace for yourself, and those are results that can be felt, seen, and heard!

# CHAPTER 4

# This is My House… I Let You Live Here

Now this parenting philosophy was a chart-topper in my household and one I'm very well acquainted with. You may not have heard this exact phrasing, but you may be familiar with some of its remixes such as: "What bill did you pay?" "You didn't pay for a [insert optional festive word here] thing in this house!" and my all-time favorite, "This is my house. You just get room and board." There were myriad ways that my dad, and likely your parents, reminded me and my siblings that the house we lived in did not belong to us. Like many of the other parenting philosophies from our childhood, this one was extremely versatile and made applicable to whatever object inside the house didn't belong to you in that moment. Didn't make your bed? *This is my house.* Shut the door a little too loudly? *This is my house* or "I know you didn't just slam *my* door!" Left a light on? *This is my house* or "Oh, so you paying the light bill now, huh?" Don't even think about getting up the nerve to ask if you could paint a wall or hang up a poster in your bedroom. *This is my house* or, "So you think you're going to just tear up the walls in *my* house?" Don't get me wrong. I understand the point they were trying to make. They worked hard for the things they had and wanted those things to be presented well and maintained to their standards. They had enough financial obligations and would prefer that those people who could not help them meet the obligations would at least not compound them. The thing was, in this context, "those people" were their children, and constantly being reminded that nothing in my house belonged to me made *me* feel like the obligation. My house was not my home. It was just the place my parents allowed me to live—the place where my dad appeared to merely tolerate my presence, a place where I did not belong.

It's funny how it never seemed to be just my dad's house when it was time to do chores. Think about the impact that it has on a child when you constantly reinforce the idea that what you're expecting them to maintain doesn't even belong to them. It does not foster pride of ownership but rather a sense of resentment. I know that's the effect it had on me, and I couldn't wait to move out of my parents' house. In fact, I did so two weeks before I even graduated high school. Still, as the saying goes, the girl can move out of the house, but the childhood trauma will reside in her forever. No? Is that not how it goes? Well, moving on… Even though I did not like how *this is my house* made me feel, it didn't stop this philosophical pattern from being repeated with my own kids once I became a parent.

I have been very intentional about creating an environment and using language that reinforces my own parenting philosophy: *our house, our home.* However, the first time one of my young sons jumped on the couch, it very quickly became "my couch" and they had just as quickly "lost their [festive] minds." When my youngest son left his action figures lying on the living room floor, it was amazing how fast they turned into his toys being on "my floor." When my oldest son wanted to do a craft or science experiment on the dining room table, I may or may not have expressed my concern about him "tearing up my table." Spoiler alert: I did. The worst part was that I could hear myself saying it, but I couldn't stop it from coming out of my mouth. I know how hurtful it was for me to hear this as a child, and I hated that I was doing the same to my kids. I never wanted them to feel like they didn't belong. I always wanted them to feel like a valued and equally important member of *our home*, whether they paid bills or not. Humans were designed to be valued and treated as significant, and when we're not, our spirits can be broken.[4] I knew I didn't want to break my sons' spirits, but I didn't know how to break this generational pattern. So I went to the Book (Manual).

Luke chapter 2 tells us the story of when Joseph and Mary lost Jesus for a few days. When Jesus was twelve years old, His parents traveled to Jerusalem for the Passover Festival as they did every year. When the festival was over, His parents were returning home when they noticed that Jesus was missing. They ultimately went back to Jerusalem to look for Him, and after three days of searching, they found Him in the temple courts listening to the teachers and asking them questions. When His parents saw this, they asked why Jesus had put them through the agony of frantically searching for Him. Jesus replied, "Why were you searching for me? Didn't you know I had to be in my Father's house?" (Luke 2:49). This story of Jesus as a young boy, not much older than my sons are now, spoke to me so clearly. The first thing I noticed was how matter-of-factly Jesus responded to His mother's question, "Didn't you know I would be in my Father's house?" On a surface level, "my Father's house" can seem very similar to our parents' version of "my house." The distinction here is that Jesus felt very comfortable and welcomed at His Father's house; He felt like He belonged there. The revelation God gave me about this passage of Scripture was in Jesus being found sitting among the teachers who were amazed by Jesus's understanding (Luke 2:47). In a place that would usually be reserved for adults, a safe space had been created for a child. I know it was a safe space because Jesus, at the tender age of twelve, was permitted to ask questions among these scholars who engaged with Him for at least three days. Their astonishment of His answers was further evidence that He belonged there in His Father's house, in His house. Fostering this sense of value and significance to His Father carried on into adulthood.

In Matthew chapter 21, an adult Jesus returned to the temple in Jerusalem and found people defiling it. As He flipped their tables over and drove people out, He reminded them, "It is written... 'My

---

[4]  See Dr. Emerson Eggerichs, *Love & Respect in the Family* (Nashville: W Publishing Group, 2013) 15.

house will be called a house of prayer', but you are making it a 'den of robbers'" (v. 13). This time it wasn't just His Father's house but His house, the place He had always felt He belonged, and we belong too. Jesus tells us in John chapter 14 that His Father's house has many rooms, and He is going to prepare a place for us (v. 2). When He comes back, He will take us with Him to the place where we belong, the house of His Father—our Father. If this is how God views the relationship between His children and His house, then I should too. That didn't mean I was going to let my kids go nuts and use "our couch" as a trampoline. What that did mean is that I had to find a way to establish parameters for what was acceptable without devaluing their sense of belonging. Like the Holy Spirit loves to do, the opportunity to practice *our house, our home* presented itself as I was writing this chapter.

My youngest son was once again playing with his action figures, which involves a lot of sound effects, tossing toys around, and loud and crashing sounds. After a particularly large crash, I felt the *this is my house* spirit rising inside of me. Instead, I looked at my son, who was already looking at me and told him that I understood he was just playing and having fun, but throwing his toys like that could end up damaging our walls and anything else they hit. I went on to affirm that this was our house and all of us would need to take care of it to keep it nice. He understood and adjusted his level of play. Now I'm not naive enough to believe that I'll never have to have this conversation with my son again. What I do believe is that I was able to convey the importance of taking care of our home without making my child feel as if he didn't belong in it.

My *our house, our home* philosophy may not be the move for you, but if you're currently applying any variation of the *this is my house* philosophy, I encourage you to reevaluate how well it's working for you *and* your kids. If you really check in with them about it, chances are you will find they feel the same way I felt as a kid. I'm not saying my philosophy is the best way, but I am saying there may be a better way for your family. When you find what works best for you, you may also find your children at peace in *their* house.

# CHAPTER 5

# Stop Crying before I Give You Something to Cry About

This parenting philosophy was a Billboard top 10 staple during my younger years. It wasn't always number 1, but it stayed in heavy rotation until I was in middle school, which is when I finally mastered the "stop crying" part, especially around my dad. Never mind that he had just lectured me for fifteen minutes straight while calling me out my name and threatening to spank me. I better not cry, or that threat would become a promise. The crazy part was that some days I would rather have just taken a whoopin'. At least then the lecture and name-calling would be over, and I'd be justified in my crying. Who am I kidding? Even crying for too long after a whoopin' could earn you another *stop crying before I give you something to cry about.* Rinse and repeat. The thing about telling your kids to stop crying when they are upset, hurt, scared, or even fearful of the consequences of their own actions is that you're teaching them that they need to suppress their emotions or, worse, that *their* emotions aren't valid. At least that's what it taught me. I learned that it was okay for my dad to be angry, upset, or frustrated with me and express his emotions accordingly, but it was not okay for me to have an emotional response to that, especially if that response involved crying. I learned not to cry, but I also learned I was not allowed to.

Now my closest friends will all tell you that I am the crybaby of the group. Don't let there be a heartwarming commercial on TV or a powerful worship song sung at church—they will look at me to see if I'm boo-hoo crying. I usually am. However, those tears are happy tears or the Spirit moving me. Those tears are okay. It was the sad tears, mad tears, or tears of frustration that became taboo. For me, crying is a cathartic experience. It allows me to release the emotions I have welling up inside of me, whether positive or negative. Being raised under a philosophy that did not permit the release of my negative emotions meant I had to keep them bottled up. Keeping those emotions forced down meant that they would eventually erupt. Instead of learning to process my emotions, I learned to mask them until I couldn't. I also developed a very strong aversion to other people's "negative tears." If I couldn't cry, neither could they. This aversion was one I carried with me into adulthood and even into my parenting.

It's very easy for us to believe that if we aren't applying a philosophy the same way our parents did, we are not perpetuating it. That is a lie, and it comes from the pit of hell. The truth about generational patterns is that while they share the same root cause, they can manifest differently in each generation. Just look at King David and his son, Solomon. David committed adultery with Bathsheba. David's adultery was the manifestation of a root of lust. Eventually, David married Bathsheba, and she bore him a son, Solomon. Solomon had seven hundred wives compared to his father's eight wives. God specifically instructed Solomon not to marry women of certain nationalities because their religious beliefs would lead him astray, but the wisest man that ever lived was no match for the lust that ran in his bloodline, and he disobeyed God—same root, different manifestation. Now that we've established that, let's talk about how the root of *stop crying before I give you something to cry about* manifested in my parenting style. Remember my aversion to other people crying? Yeah, well it was a borderline hatred. It was less about the reasons someone might be crying or even the act itself but more the sound of crying that worked (and still works) my nerves. There is something about the way children cry that sounds like fingernails scratching a chalkboard to my ears. I suspect my dad suffered from the same affliction. As a childless young adult, I couldn't even stand hearing someone else's child cry in the store. Then I became a parent, and my kids cried and cried and didn't sleep and cried some more. Let's just say that those were some dark days compounded by my aversion to the sound of crying—an aversion rooted in a parenting philosophy from my childhood.

While I've never told my kids to stop crying in the same way, my body language, facial expressions, and energy, in general, conveyed the same message loud and clear: It is *not* acceptable to cry, especially when you're mad, sad, hurting, or frustrated. I never wanted my kids to feel that way. I hated feeling that way. One of the many reasons I'm in therapy now is because of a whole life spent feeling that way, yet here we were—same root, different manifestation. I could see my kids trying so hard not to cry it would cause them headaches. At least then, Mommy would care for them instead of being annoyed by them. Causing my children to internalize their emotions only meant they would eventually spill over in an often-hysterical way. I was self-aware enough to know what I was doing, even in the moment, but I didn't know how to change the pattern. It was time to consult the Manual.

The Bible has a lot to say about crying. There are many verses that assert the acceptability of crying and reassure us that God hears our cries. At the end of the day, we all just want to know that when we cry, there is someone who hears us and cares. One such person was a woman named Hannah. Hannah's story can be found in 1 Samuel. She was married to Elkanah, who had a second wife named Peninnah. Peninnah bore Elkanah many children, but Hannah had none. Because God had closed Hannah's womb, Elkanah loved her all the more. Because Elkanah showed favoritism toward Hannah, Peninnah hated and provoked her. This treatment went on for years and eventually brought Hannah to tears and crying before the Lord. The first person to tell Hannah to *stop crying* was her husband. "Hannah, why are you weeping? Why are you downhearted? Don't I mean more to you than ten sons?" (1 Samuel 1:8). Talk about adding insult to injury! Hannah's husband knew the reasons for her tears all too well, but instead of validating her emotions, he dismissed them by implying that his subsequent feelings of inadequacy took precedence. After all, the joy of being married to Elkanah was worth more than the grief brought on by not being able to bare any children. It's important to understand that, in Hannah's society, a woman who could not bear children, especially a son to carry on the family lineage, had no value. So Hannah took her petition to the Lord directly.

Weeping bitterly, she prayed for God to give her a son and vowed that she would give him back to the Lord. As she continued to cry and pray inaudibly, the priest Eli approached her with a second request to *stop crying*. "How long are you going to stay drunk? Put away your wine" (1 Samuel 1:14). Random, but don't you love puns? I think Eli might have used the first recorded pun in history. Hannah and her family had been engaging in their annual sacrifice to the Lord at the temple, which also included eating food and drinking wine. Eli told Hannah to put away her wine, but I think he really meant whine. Eli's focus was on the what (crying) and not the why. Hannah's release of emotion was uncomfortable, disruptive, and inconvenient to those that should have had the most empathy and sympathy for her. Hannah replied to Eli that she was not drunk, nor had she even been drinking but was pouring out her soul to the Lord out of her great anguish. When Eli realized *why* Hannah was crying, he told her to go in peace and came into agreement with Hannah and her request of God. Hannah's husband told her to *stop crying*. Hannah's priest told her to *stop crying*. However, Hannah's heavenly Father heard her cry. He allowed space for her to release her emotions to Him because He is close to the brokenhearted (Psalm 34:18), and He will turn weeping into gladness (John 16:20). Hannah left the house of the Lord no longer downcast and later bore a son, Samuel.

As parents, we know that we won't always be able to turn our kids tears into smiles. However, we can reevaluate the way we're responding to our children's tears. Kathleen Edelman says that when we dismiss our kids' emotions, we tear them down,[5] but when we

---

[5] See Kathleen Edelman, *A Grown-Up's Guide to Kids' Wiring* (United States: Kind Words Are Cool, 2021) 222.

validate their feelings, we're responding to the why rather than react-ing to the what. Instead of reacting to crying with a *stop crying*, try to address what triggered the tears. If your communication with or treatment of your child was the trigger, it may also be time to evaluate whether the parenting philosophies of your childhood are contribut-ing to a negative generational pattern being repeated with your kids. Being intentional about acknowledging, addressing, and adjusting these philosophies to something that works better for you and your children can lead to more peace, and that's definitely something to shed a few happy tears about!

# CHAPTER 6

# I Brought You into This World and I'll Take You Out!

This parenting philosophy was my mom's version of Nas's Ether in my childhood (I most definitely just aged myself). This was the track that shut everything down. There was no response to it. To be fair, it did usually come after me or my siblings fell completely out of line with one of the aforementioned parenting philosophies or majorly violated one of the various other rules of our household. This was the heater she brought out when she had been pushed to her limit by our disobedience or insubordination. Now that I'm a parent, I fully understand the level of frustration and exhaustion you have to be at to threaten your children's demise in exchange for a little peace and quiet, but when I was a child, it wasn't just a threat to me. A much younger Crystal fully believed that stepping too far out of line gave my mom the right to end my life. After all, she had given it to me. There is so much to unpack about this particular philosophy.

First is the extreme nature of the consequence. Ceasing to exist was presented as a commensurate response to breaking a rule or violating a boundary in a big enough way. Dr. Gary Chapman and Dr. Ross Campbell say that punishments must fit the crime, be appropriate for the particular child, and planned ahead by the parent to avoid falling into the "punishment trap" like the one this philosophy would suggest.[6] As I got older, I knew my mother did not literally mean she would take my life, but the fact that she would even suggest it taught me that extreme responses were valid when your emotions were high. This extreme emotional response is something I've had to work very hard to overcome in my adult life.

Second is the extreme expression of authority. When the options being presented are to fall in line or die, the child they're being presented to is left with very little sense of control or choice in the matter. In her book on *The Way They Learn*, Cynthia Ulrich Tobias says that children expect their parents to be in authority but that a parent's greatest challenge is in how they communicate that authority.[7] For some children, limiting their sense of control will cause them to limit their cooperation with the boundaries you've set for them. It's almost like daring them to step over the line you've established and call your bluff. I know my sister took it as a personal challenge when we were kids. When given the choice between no control and "death," she chose death almost every time. Just in case you were wondering, she's still alive today.

Third is the hostile devaluation of life and being. In his book *Mother & Son: The Respect Effect*, Dr. Emerson Eggerichs says that hostility and contempt not only make a child feel bad but can warp their self-image.[8] Some parents, especially those who did not receive much love in their own childhood, tend to focus their parenting on these less-positive forms of discipline and skip the importance of nurturing their children.[9] Consider what it must feel like for a child to have their own parent suggest that their life is expendable. It doesn't matter that they were angry or upset in the moment and didn't mean it literally, threatening a child in this way can kill their

---

6   See Gary Chapman and Ross Campbell, *The 5 Love Languages of Children* (Chicago: Northfield Publishing, 2012) 137.

7   See Cynthia Ulrich Tobias, *The Way They Learn* (Carol Stream: Tyndale House Publishers, 1994) 63.

8   See Dr. Emerson Eggerichs, *Mother & Son: The Respect Effect* (Nashville: W Publishing Group, 2016) 205.

9   See Gary Chapman and Ross Campbell, *The 5 Love Languages of Children* (Chicago: Northfield Publishing, 2012) 126.

self-confidence, self-worth, and leave them questioning their place of importance to the people most important to them: their parents.

Finally, this philosophy is contradictory to the principles of God. The Bible is very clear when it comes to God's stance on the treatment of children, caring for those who cannot care for themselves, oh, and murder. The Bible is also very clear that it is God and not parents who bring children into this world. Sure, He uses parents as vessels and then stewards of the children He entrusts to them, but it is Him who forms each child in their mother's womb and sets them apart before they are even born (Jeremiah 1:5). Only God has the power to take us out of this world because He is our Creator. God is the ultimate authority and that leaves the stewards of His children only with the power of choice. Those choices include the philosophies by which they choose to parent. I can think of another parent in the Bible who was presented with a similar life or death choice concerning his child.

I'm sure most of you are familiar with the story of Abraham and Sarah. For those that aren't, the Cliff's Notes version is that Abraham and Sarah waited a long time and went through a lot of (self-induced) drama to finally have a child. Their son Isaac was the fulfillment of the promises God had given them. So it must have been quite jarring when God later asked Abraham to kill his only son (Genesis 22:2). The child that he had waited a lifetime for, the manifestation of God's promise, was to be sacrificed back to the Lord. It couldn't have been me! Abraham, however, was immediately obedient to God's command. The next morning, he set out with his son toward the mountain where God instructed the sacrifice to take place. As Isaac and Abraham traveled up the mountain, Isaac started to question where the lamb for the sacrifice was. Abraham assured him God would provide. When they got to the top of the mountain, Abraham bound Isaac and placed him on the altar for the sacrifice. As he drew his knife to kill Isaac, an angel called out telling Abraham not to lay a hand on or hurt the boy. Abraham's choice was not whether he should take his kid out of this world or not. That choice belongs to God alone. Abraham's choice was whether he would be obedient to God's will or not. That meant doing his best to honor the principles

God had given him and being the best steward he could be to the gift God gave him in Isaac. Abraham did not desire to harm his child and He trusted God would provide a solution to that end. I know that my mom did not desire to hurt me, not truly, but even the implication that the person who was supposed to care for me the most would be responsible for my end did harm me in unseen ways. It harmed my sense of value and the level of trust I had in those who were supposed to care for me. I never wanted to repeat that harm with my children. I pray God never asks of me what He asked of Abraham that day. I use this particular story from the Bible because I want to highlight something we discussed in an earlier chapter of this book: the power of choice or as us churchy folk might say, free will.

I can say that I've never repeated this parenting philosophy with my children. Though there have absolutely been times that I have been tired, weary, and generally annoyed enough to have had this response, I have never let these words come out of my mouth. There are several reasons why. First, I understand just how terrible hearing this from your parent can make you feel. I never want to give my children the impression that, because they are children, their lives are less valuable. I also never want to deceive myself into believing that because I'm their parent I can exercise control over them with no limits. Both these ideas are false. The truth is our children are an embodiment of God's promises to us, just as Isaac was to Abraham and Sarah. They are extremely precious to God, and as their stewards, we should handle them with care. That doesn't mean there won't be times that we feel like we're at our wit's end with our kids, but we have the power to choose how we respond, and there are so many examples in our manual that show us how to do so in a way that's in accordance with God's will.

I have found that my amazingly intuitive little boys can tell when I'm at my limit, and often they are the ones that bring that realization to me in the moment. "Mommy, are you having a tough day today?" "Mommy, are you stressed?" "Mommy, why are you so grumpy?" When those moments arise and their questions follow, it is my opportunity to choose my response. I have chosen to engage in conversation with them by first acknowledging what my behavior is already expressing and then explaining to them why I feel that way. If their behavior has contributed to those feelings, I am honest about that too. This is not about letting your kids off the hook or letting them run wild or run over you. This is about teaching them how to handle these feelings themselves and doing so in a way that doesn't cause them harm. Some of these conversations are hard to have because it forces you to confront the truth about your own behavior and/or the root of the particular set of parenting philosophies you're operating under. I encourage you to have them anyway. Just do so in a way that works the best for you and your children. I truly believe that when you make *that* choice, it will lead to increased peace for you, your kids, and your household. Over time, the narrative will change from threatening to take your kids out of this world to expressing and them truly believing that you could never imagine your world without them!

# CHAPTER 7

# Who the Son Sets Free
# Is Free Indeed

We've covered a lot in such a short book. Some of you may be reliving your childhood experiences with these philosophies and are relating to me far more than you'd like to right now. Others of you may have no earthly idea what I have been talking about for the last several pages or so. Whichever category you fall into, I think it's safe to say all of us who are now parents grew up under certain principles or beliefs that we didn't like and which affected us profoundly. The ones in this book were just a few examples of mine, but whatever the philosophies of your childhood were, I encourage you to examine both them and yourself. Were these philosophies in line with the values and principles of God? If not, are you repeating a potentially negative pattern by using them with your own children? The answer might be "no" for you, but for me, the answer was a surprising "yes." Surprising because I know how much they affected me growing up. Equally surprising was how easily I fell into using the same philosophies when I became a parent. You truly never know how you're going to respond until a situation presents itself and you're presented with a choice.

When I made the decision to go back to therapy, the reason I told my therapist I was there was to learn how to better communicate with my children. As I said earlier, parenthood is a spiritual war, and I had gotten to a place where I felt like I was losing more battles than winning. I felt like the techniques I was using with my kids weren't effective. I felt like I had no control over the situation, and in turn, I had no peace. Worse than all those things, I felt like my kids didn't feel loved by me. Articulating that thought brought me to tears, the sad kind. I was very clear from the start that I didn't want my kids to feel the same way I had felt at times growing up. I knew the likely negative effects of this. I had lived them. They had brought me to this moment in my parenting journey. I prayed. I fasted. I commiserated with other parents. I received a lot of well-intentioned advice. I received an equal amount of judgment. I pleaded with God. Still, there was not much improvement; still more losses than wins. I needed help. I assumed that my therapist, an amazing woman of God, would give me a magical blueprint on how I could better communicate with my kids—ya know, a few infinity stones and the snap-of-the-finger kind of technique. I wanted to know the secret to how I could regain control of my life, my peace, and ensure my children felt loved. Instead, she asked me about my relationship with my parents.

Many of those first sessions were spent talking about my childhood and how my parents communicated with me during that time. As we continued to discuss my past, I saw so clearly the effect it was having on my present. If I wanted my future to be different, I was going to have to do a different thing now. It's never too late to try a new thing, especially when it comes to parenting. Even if your children are grown and out on their own, acknowledging the parenting philosophies that didn't work and trying new ones can help improve your communication with your adult children and improve your relationships with your grandchildren. You are receiving this revelation now because you are ready to receive it now, for such a time as this!

Trying a new thing isn't always easy. There can be a lot of trial and error to find what works for you and your kids. However, if what you've been doing isn't working, isn't a new thing worth a shot? What helped and continues to help me on my journey of trying something different is setting the appropriate expectations for the outcome. At the end of the day, a parent cannot control what their child chooses to do. It is the child who must decide to choose a parents' values.[10] They have free will. What a parent *can* control is choosing to align their parenting philosophies *and* responses to their children's disobedience with the principles and values of God. Setting my expectations accordingly removed the pressure for the next thing I tried to be the thing that worked, and it allowed me the freedom to keep trying until I found the thing that did. I also had to remind myself of one important truth: I was equipped for this.

God would not have entrusted my specific children to me if He had not already given me everything I needed to steward them well. Parents are Christ's vessels and the Lord's primary means of implanting instruction in our kids.[11] It is our job to teach our children about love and respect, so our parenting philosophies must be rooted in both. Our kids are not an obligation we have to tolerate. They are a reward and a heritage from the Lord (Psalm 127:3). When we communicate with and parent our children in ways that convey we love, respect, and view them as gifts, they can become one of our most effective weapons in this war we call parenthood. Remember, our battles are spiritual. The Bible says children are like arrows in the hands of a warrior and calls the man whose quiver is full of them blessed (Psalm 127:4–5).

Unlearning the parenting philosophies of my childhood and implementing ones that work better for me and my kids will help stop some of the negative generational patterns that have persisted in my family bloodline. That's a huge victory in one of the most consequential battles of this war. It's one less battle that my sons will have to fight when they grow up and become parents. Together, we are creating a new pattern that will positively affect our family for the generations that follow. Being prepared for war is one of the most effective means of preserving peace. Know that the enemy would love nothing more than to use us as weapons in the mass destruction

---

[10] See Dr. Emerson Eggerichs, *Mother & Son: The Respect Effect* (Nashville: W Publishing Group, 2016) 44.

[11] See Dr. Emerson Eggerichs, *Love & Respect in the Family* (Nashville: W Publishing Group, 2013) 82.

of our children's spirits and lives. I wrote a book about that too.[12] We have the power to choose whether our parenting philosophies will be of service to him or God. Choose wisely because that choice may be the determining factor in winning this war!

_______________

[12] See Crystal Wright Adams, *Perversion of Love: Understanding the Enemy's Attack on Your Love Language* (Meadville: Christian Faith Publishing, 2021).

# ABOUT THE AUTHOR

Crystal lives in San Antonio, Texas, with her two amazing sons. Her passion for community and service led her to cofound a nonprofit teenage girls' mentoring organization called Caterpillars to Butterflies (C2B). That same passion for community, service, and mentoring led her to answer God's call to write about family dynamics, often using her personal experiences.

Crystal has a bachelor of arts in communication studies from the University of Texas at San Antonio, a graduate certificate in pastoral counseling from Liberty University, and a certificate in nonprofit management from Cornell University. She loves Jesus, her family, and basketball! Go, Dubs! She can often be found having a movie night with her sons or watching any level of competitive basketball.

Crystal's first book, *Perversion of Love*, further explores the parent-child relationship and its effects on how adults come to understand, receive, and give love. Her writing is also featured in an anthology entitled *She Changed Her Narrative*. Both works are currently available through Amazon and Barnes & Noble, and be on the lookout for more to come!